An Envelope Waiting

poems by

Lisa Roullard

Finishing Line Press
Georgetown, Kentucky

An Envelope Waiting

Copyright © 2020 by Lisa Roullard
ISBN 978-1-64662-300-6 First Edition
All rights reserved under International and Pan-American Copyright Conventions.
No part of this book may be reproduced in any manner whatsoever without written permission from the publisher, except in the case of brief quotations embodied in critical articles and reviews.

ACKNOWLEDGMENTS

Grateful acknowledgement is made to the editors of publications in which these poems first appeared, sometimes in different versions:

Atlanta Review: "Postage Stamps, the First Date Series: Origami, the Kitchen Table"
Broadkill Review: "When I Am an Envelope, White #10" and "When I Am a Letter"
The Cabin: "Postage Stamps, the First Date Series: Below Train Tracks, Bellingham, Washington"
Fugue and *Verse Daily:* "Postage Stamps, the First Date Series: Watching the Kingdome Implosion Broadcast, Seattle, Washington"
Helicon West Anthology: "The Mailman and the Pear Tree"
Hubbub: "Skinny-Dipping, with Mailman"
Talking River: "The Mailman at the Pool" and "The Mailman in Motion"

"The Mailman in the Forest," "The Mailman in the Bathtub," and "When I Am a Stamp" appeared in poemballs with Provo Poetry

Publisher: Leah Maines
Editor: Christen Kincaid
Cover Art: Cat Palmer, catpalmer.com
Author Photo: Cat Palmer, catpalmer.com
Cover Design: Elizabeth Maines McCleavy

Order online: www.finishinglinepress.com
also available on amazon.com

Author inquiries and mail orders:
Finishing Line Press
P. O. Box 1626
Georgetown, Kentucky 40324
U. S. A.

Table of Contents

Skinny-Dipping, with Mailman 1

The Mailman in the Forest 2

When I Am an Envelope, White #10 3

The Mailman in the Bathtub 4

Postage Stamps, the First Date Series: Below Train Tracks,
Bellingham, Washington 5

The Mailman at the Pool 6

Postage Stamps, the First Date Series: A Wine Bar, Spokane,
Washington 7

The Mailman in the Carport 8

Postage Stamp Set, the First Date Series: Spokane,
Washington 9

Letter Never Written But Still Surfacing 10

When I Am a Stamp 11

When I Am a Mailbox 12

Postage Stamps, the First Date Series: Gasworks Parks,
Seattle, Washington 13

The Mailman in Motion 14

Postage Stamps, the First Date Series: Origami, the Kitchen
Table 15

Postage Stamps, the First Date Series: Watching the Kingdome
Implosion Broadcast, Seattle, Washington 16

When I Am a Letter 17

The Mailman and the Pear Tree 18

For all letter writers—past, present, and future

Skinny-Dipping, with Mailman

Quarry lake, end of the pot-holed road, and a girl skinny-dipping.
Something to be mailed—that possibility. And she is—
her sundress an envelope waiting.

Strawberry-blond, freckle-limbed: she's the letter composed

in someone's head—the mailman's maybe. He's seated
on granite that's warming, apple clasped by left hand.
The right flips crisp magazines.

Neither knows the other. Nor notices. She slips through bluest green.

When a letter's sent, mom, auntie, lover can't always know
it's coming. That fluttering thrill. Girlhood,
summer, and the freedom of the to-be written.

The *Dear, How are you?* unobserved, naked, swimming.

The Mailman in the Forest

A kind of uncertainty, of intention, of no GPS.
The mailman has his mail shoes
and he is on foot. He supports his safari-esque hat.

>These are the woods, reaching and damp.
>The details could bite you alive.

>>Here, in a swath of white-water cold, a bird walks
>>underwater upstream. He swims too, for prey.
>>Slate-colored, this dipper, who bobs
>>from rocks, outsinging
>>the singing river.

Does the mailman have the mail? You cannot see the truck.
Light meanders evergreen. No route,
like a Sunday. No boxes or slots.

When I Am an Envelope, White #10

I will keep a space. A flat pocket
my gift to give, obvious
and secret.

Consider the seashell with a twist:
exactly where it spirals
into itself cannot be
completely seen.

I'll hold out hope that someone
will mail the sea.
Will it be the same,
what the waves write in my shell?

From a tunnel of pearl, the ever-roar
releasing gently.

The Mailman in the Bathtub

A place to steam letters,
he thinks, one toe about in,
door locked and the faucet hard over, the water
broth hot.

        To hold the seal there, just at the streaming tap
        could be side work. Off the route.
        Like this bath, at last.

                Opening each envelope could yield
                a tidy sigh. Self-directed
                and privileged. The little song
                of an address.

Postage Stamps, the First Date Series: Below Train Tracks, Bellingham, Washington

Creosote air, a space sized for two.
For sunken ships, he tells her,
no responsibilities remain.

Down-trail at the bay the tide subtracting.

Is this a place to bring a girl? Weight-thrown
grit. Tracks and timbers tightly tacked.
The dog you can't see, barking.

The Mailman at the Pool

       Not a route—his or any other's—this echo-catching
                space, acred, wave-blue and flicker,
    it seems
           so unlike the mail

        senior water aerobics, particularly,
                wrinkles jiggling: the water's
                      and the bodies'.
"Dancing Queen" skips
              silver-tipped
       synchronous stretch for the ceiling;

    light breathes, keeping up.

            Could this be mail?

            The Wet Letter Office?
Aerobicists lost
        in sentiment and splash
        pulse check and sidestep

    perishable, liquid, fragile
        so real as to be
                hazardous.

Postage Stamps, the First Date Series: A Wine Bar, Spokane, Washington

Yes, it's strange being titled and framed.

The man's speaking, been going on and on since
she thinks, before there was before.
He's waterfall roar. Niagara-perpetual,

leaning in to her incessant listening.

She prays for precedent: that any date who
talks so much—four generations, the same
small town—how much *is* there to say?—
can be deftly duct-taped.

(USA, Forever, and the scalloped edges.)
To carry such words in case the letter doesn't.

The Mailman in the Carport

Wednesday. The weight of ads, slick and loud
and stacked in his bag.
Slot after slot he's stuffed them in.
Scratch of mid-morning. The just-about rain.

    And here's a carport, with nothing for sale.
    A place between houses that's built
    for what moves—
    carless and sturdy and offering.

        The blue cooler's tricked out with grit,
        sawdust tracks an oil stain.
        So the mailman sits, suspends
        what he places in people's lives.

            Nothing shiny but everything true:
            pots set within each other,
            a snow shovel of leaves
            and a broken-off rake.

                This is the view from rest, mid-week.
                Past the downspout
                raindrops splat unsolicited.
                A circular delivered by spring.

**Postage Stamp Set, the First Date Series:
    Spokane, Washington**

Waiting, Riverfront Park

Like August she arrived on time,
though the bench offers no hieroglyphics,
can't name who, eventually, must
remove the umbrella-shaped trees or
offer why, at this warm, warm now
there can't be rain. A stroller. A car,
another—no—same one the other way.
An eager face; a watch, in shadow.
She is full with holding still, with staying,
as the trees do. As does the day.

Somewhere

He is the letter never mailed. Written,
yes—the page a white shirttail long
untucked—but lost, *no*, set *somewhere*
on the floor's sea: to bob, to drift.
(Dust tornadoes by in puffs.)
Five o'clock shadows; the script of an
oboe hand is stuck. Is stuck. Is.
And the clock chiming in: Who
reads what won't show up?

Letter Never Written But Still Surfacing

Envelope like an ironed dream,
a cloud, pressed and rising
from rumpled voices,
the going-on of being
where no one stops
to take their pulse:
blue beats
as certain as paper
folded in thirds;
as certain as finger, pen, heart
braided to handwriting.

Does sunlight lift
the weight?

I itch for the chance
to slip to the sealed
edge, delight in
the requisite ripping.

When I Am a Stamp

As a long, landscape rectangle I will bask, I will window.
This image and just this: aspen, aspen spiriting leaves,
frog-green, rushed into being by breeze, all lilt, lift,
shimmy-tickle. Aboard the envelope I dream

straightforward in verbs: *affix* not *stick*. *Mail,
cancel, deliver.* One job and one job only, essential,
a signature—this letter cannot become mail without me, rooted
grove of self-adhesive trees. Before the mailman, before

the recipient, the letter writer set eyes on my gentle, electric
scene and saw what my artist saw, felt
what isn't shown—sunlight on shoulders—thought of
the *one* he'd written, then pressed fingers against me.

When I Am a Mailbox

Suited to this solitude, this
stillness, I'll be practitioner
of patience, shaper of space. I'll be
a nest or a harbor galvanized,
postmaster approved.

Truth: I can't write
letters. But under the seasons'
spin I'll excel
at assistance,
it's still correspondence—the proper
tool placed in the hand.
(My trinity: sender, mailman, recipient.)

Galvanized, as I said,
may that offer protection
from firecracker and bat.
There's prayer,
I suppose, to prevent
being furloughed, that fantastic
stagnancy, or getting witched in
by decades-old hedges.

How I'll love 11074,
Puget Sound's wet turns, the mail truck's
gentle approach.
My one sweet door
from which mail slides in, slides
out like a paper tide.

And the moon stuck fast
most nights, posting the sky.
Single wing of a bird,
my flag.

Postage Stamps, the First Date Series: Gasworks Park, Seattle, Washington

At the lakeshore—turned almost
to each other, turned just now silhouette—she holds
the rolled-down bag. He tosses the bread.

    His arm, she notes, has come to an arc.

    Same up-swung shape, she's been told,
    that must backbone a story, if there's to be more
    —oh let there be more—

    than duck-like scrambling. Than stale conversation.

(And that bread in mid-air, whole wheat
hunk of star,
is momentarily rising.)

The Mailman in Motion

I could not be wind, but
I go, house to
house by heart-
beat walking, my
own weather
to move

note the street
signs with their strict,
straight green, pavement
with its firm
grumble   such
relief to propel
past the scratchy
time-scrawl
of junipers
—may they not write
on me—
mailbag pulsing
my hip
with lessening sway
as it empties

I retrieve a flock
of catalogs,
release those
tropical birds

Postage Stamps, the First Date Series:
Origami, the Kitchen Table

Penguin. Her hand teaches his
to fold—that the fingernail, once paper's edge
is where it needs to go and straight,
must commence the crease.

Left fingers poised: across them her right ones move.

Purple, red, yellow and silver
squares. Four hands, eight times, fold
and smooth. Kite-shaped for a bit, then
turquoise beak, then wings.

Postage Stamps, the First Date Series: Watching the Kingdome Implosion Broadcast, Seattle, Washington

Lips to lips; dome to bits: with centered
weight the sofa sags though not
as fast, this pair dipping, as imploding
concrete ribs and

ramps, which can't be seen—TV's

gone gray, this detonation
just as planned: neck and back
and tip and *oh* and thigh and all that
space.

When I Am a Letter

It will be proper pleasure
and I am prepared
to be black ink, self-saying.

I, too, will be the page:
forest after white
forest wandering
within edges.

There will flit the chickadee,
whistle and song
of handwriting, black-capped
and common.

There will crook the stream,
sunlit in spots,
a surfacing vein.

But in this forest, letter
alive, there will flick
the ravenous,
the unraveling.

The tree struck by lightning
will strike me too:
vulnerable and solid.
Charred and stark and upright.

I will write with that char,
left-handed as the heart
which often smears
what it has to say.

The Mailman and the Pear Tree

He'd realized only tree,
not pears,
so wasn't deep enough in his knee-bend
to pass under freely,
his blue mail shirt
like a second sky
swinging up to the branches.

And the pears,
little riddles of women,
gold-green and etch-speckled,
announced themselves
like stealthy percussion,
one fruit plunking
in the mouth of the mailbag
pear Avion.
Warm. Unnoticed.

In the leafy edges of air
the mailman stops,
sidesteps and straightens.

Each pear so unlike
an envelope,
he thinks, as some wait
near his street-worn shoes
and more above him sway.
Yet each arrives
sealed and stored with messages,
one from each seed's letter:
the ripening hope
of trees.

Born and raised in Seattle, **Lisa Roullard** holds an MFA from Eastern Washington University. Her poetry has been nominated for the Pushcart Prize and has appeared in various magazines as well as on busses in Boise, Idaho, as part of Poetry in Motion. In 2013 she won the Utah Original Writing Competition for poetry. She lives in Salt Lake City, Utah, with her family. As often as possible she walks in the rain.

www.ingramcontent.com/pod-product-compliance
Lightning Source LLC
LaVergne TN
LVHW041525070426
835507LV00013B/1822